Christian
Church

Angela Gluck Wood

W

FRANKLIN WATTS
LONDON • SYDNEY

This is the symbol used to
represent the Christian faith.

For Jennifer, Caroline, David and Joshua

This edition first published 2005

Franklin Watts
96 Leonard Street
London EC2A 4XD

Franklin Watts Australia
45-51 Huntley Street
Alexandria NSW2015

© Franklin Watts 1998

Editor: Samantha Armstrong
Series Designer: Kirstie Billingham
Illustrator: Gemini Patel
Religious Education Consultant: Margaret Barratt M.A., Religious Education Lecturer
Christianity Consultant: Alison Seaman, Deputy Director, National Society Religious Education Centre
Reading Consultant: Prue Goodwin, Reading and Language Information Centre, Reading

Dewey Decimal Classification Number 230

A CIP catalogue record for this book is available from
the British Library

ISBN 0 7496 6208 5

Printed in China

Contents

Churches around the world

A **church** is a place where Christians go to worship God. There are many different kinds of Christian worship. There are churches all around the world.

This is a modern ▶ church.

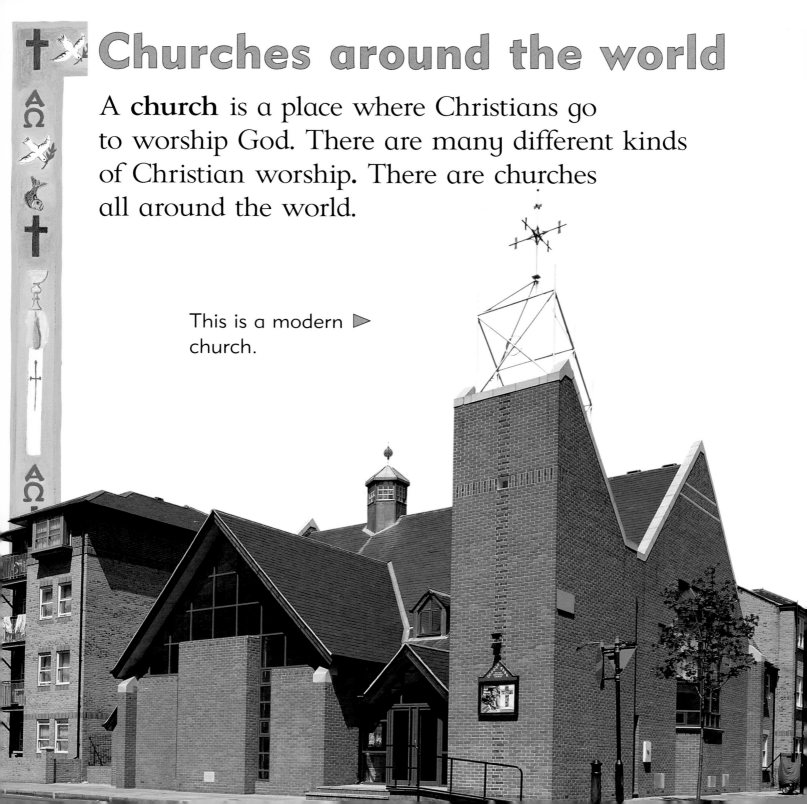

Christian belief

Christians believe in one God who created the world. He loved people so much that he sent his son, Jesus to live among them.

◁ This is Jesus with his mother, Mary.

7

Jesus

Jesus lived on earth and helped people to understand about God. He taught people how to live together lovingly. Many of them did not understand who he was or the things he did. Because of this he was killed on a **cross**. Some churches have a statue of Jesus on a cross. This is called a **crucifix**.

When Christians see a ▷ crucifix they remember that Jesus loved them enough to die for them.

Most churches have a plain cross. Christians believe that three days after Jesus was buried he was alive again and with his followers. The cross tells Christians that Jesus did not die forever and that he is with them always.

There are often candles ▷ in churches. They remind Christians that Jesus was like a light to guide them.

9

Inside a church

Churches can be plain or they can have a lot of pictures and objects with different meanings in them. Often a **priest, minister** or **preacher** leads the worship at the front of the church.

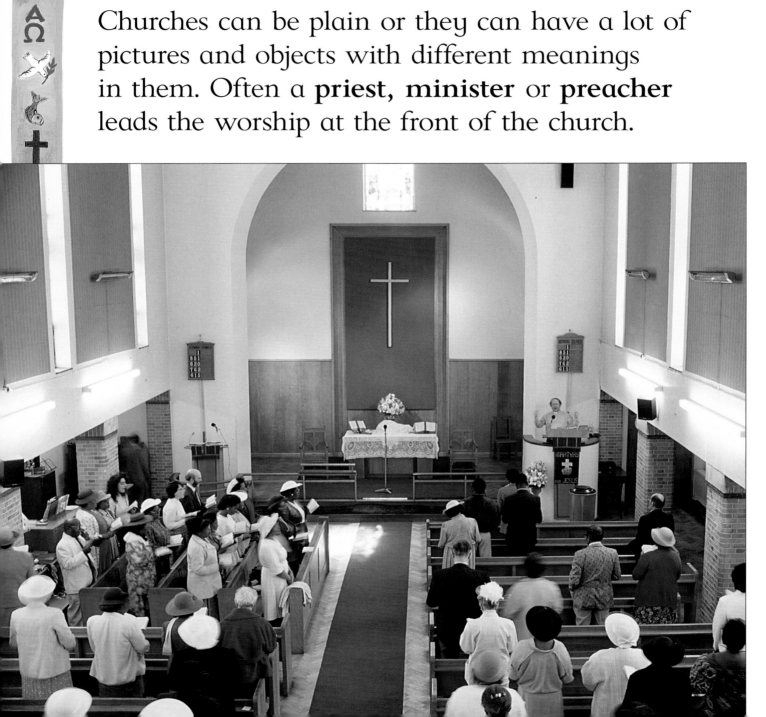

The altar

Most churches have an **altar** or a **communion table** in a place where everyone can see it.
It reminds Christians of the last meal that Jesus had with his followers, the Last Supper, when he told them he would always be with them.

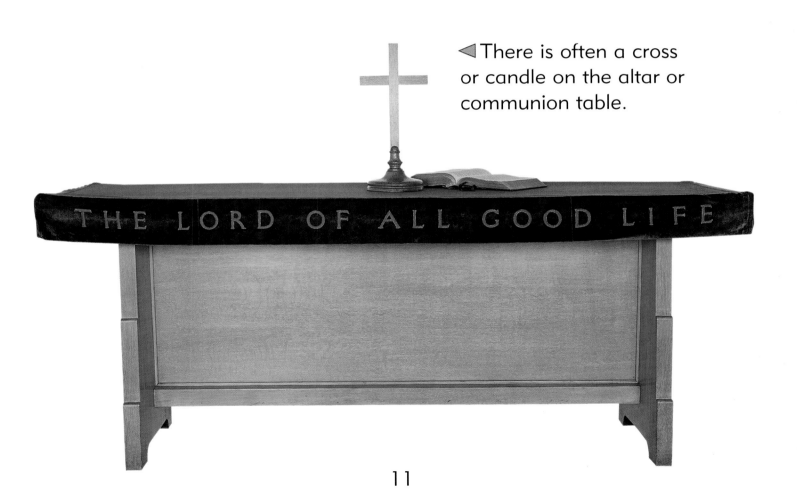

◀ There is often a cross or candle on the altar or communion table.

THE LORD OF ALL GOOD LIFE

The Bible

There are always Bibles in a church.
The **Bible** is the most important Christian book.
It tells Christians about how God guided
people before Jesus was born. It also describes
Jesus, his teachings and the beginning of
the church. Many Christians have their own Bibles.

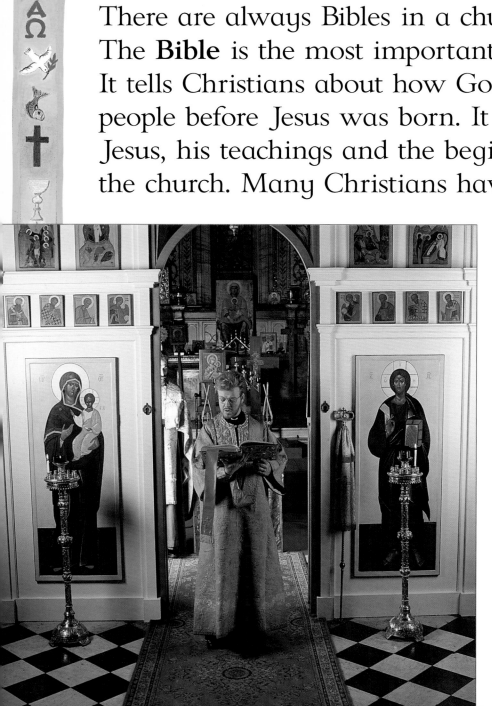

◁ This Orthodox
minister, or deacon,
is reading the
Bible to the
congregation.

The Bible is ▷
often read from
a stand called
a lectern.
This priest is
kissing the Bible
to show his love
for God's words.

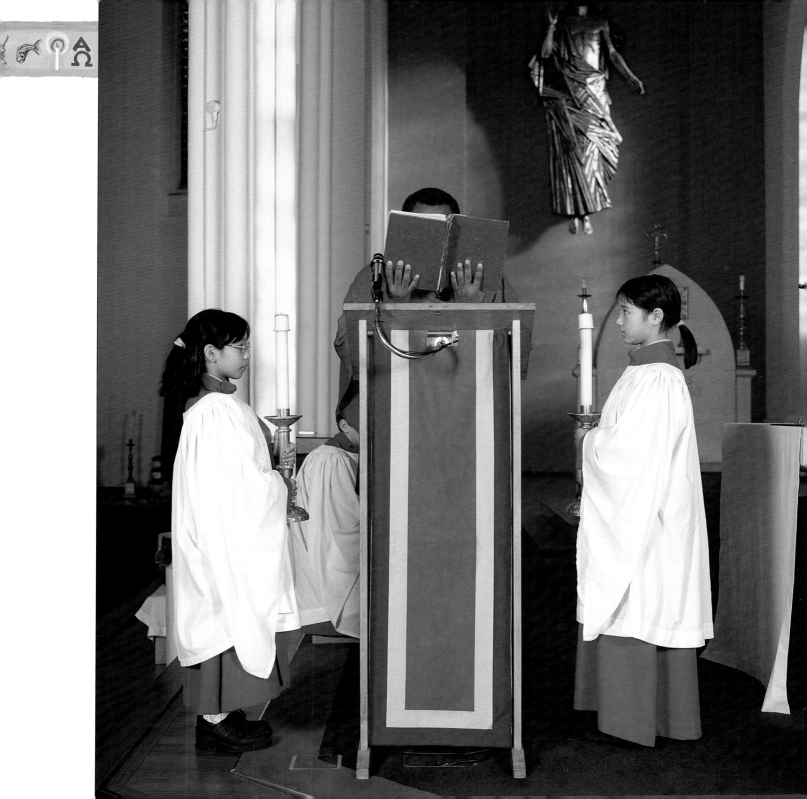

The sermon

The preacher usually explains what the Bible means to Christians today. The talk is called a **sermon.**

The sermon helps ▷
Christians to think
about what they believe.

Windows

Some churches have beautiful windows with pictures made out of stained glass. They often tell stories from the Bible or show **saints.** (Saints are people who show their love for Jesus in special ways.)

This window shows ▷ St. John the Baptist baptizing Jesus before he began teaching.

15

Being part of the church

People often start life as a Christian by being **baptized**. This means they are **blessed** with **holy** water.
In a church the water is often held in a **font**.

This Catholic woman blesses ▷ herself with holy water as she comes into a church. It tells her that God is there.

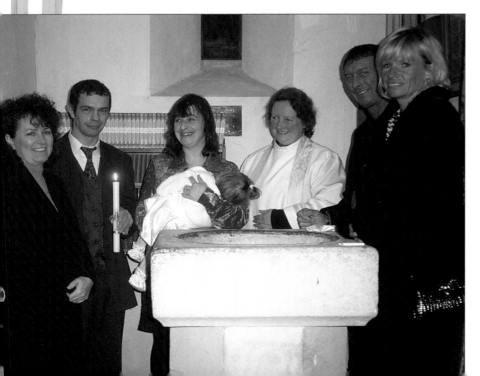

◁ Christians are baptized when they are grown up or as babies. This baby is being baptized at a font.

Christians feel that God is always with them. They call this the **Holy Spirit**. The Holy Spirit shows them how to love and help others. In some churches the Holy Spirit is shown as a dove or pictures of flames.

One way that Christians help ▷ others is by giving money to those in need. Often this is collected in the church.

◁ The dove stands for the Holy Spirit coming into the world. The circle is the world.

17

A church service

The special day for most Christians is Sunday. Many churches have **services** on Sundays. This is when Christians gather together to share their love for God. In some churches there are lots of people and music plays an important part in the service. In others it is very quiet and still.

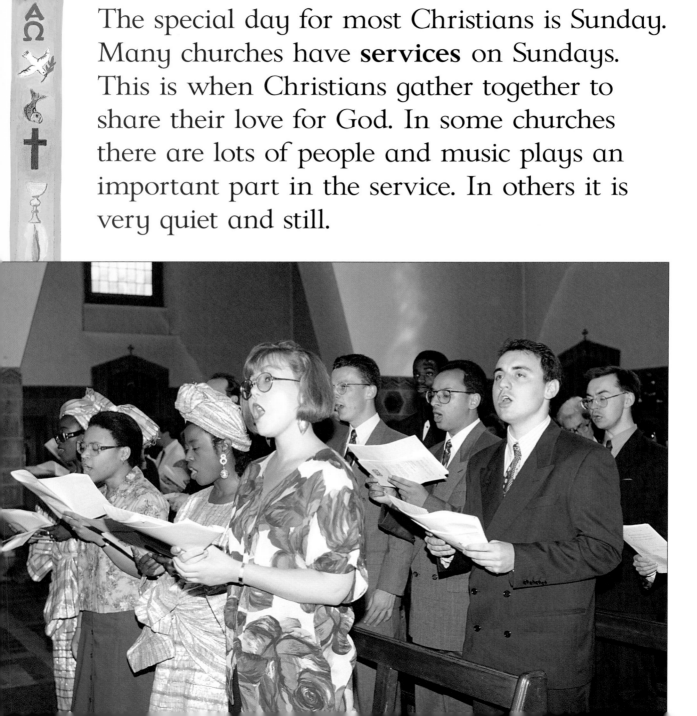

◀ These children
are sitting together
in the church as
they pray to God.

As part of a service, people say **prayers.**
Prayers are a way that Christians speak
and listen to God. Usually someone reads
from the Bible. Everyone joins together
to sing **hymns** that praise God.
In some churches a **choir** leads the
hymn singing.

Holy Communion

Some churches have a service called **Holy Communion**. The people eat a piece of bread and drink some wine or grape juice to remember the Last Supper (see page 11).

The minister blesses the bread and wine.
Then the people eat and drink them.
They think about how Jesus loves them.

 # Mass

In some churches, for example a Roman Catholic church, Holy Communion is called **Mass**. The priest uses wine and a wafer of special bread. Each wafer is called a **host**.

◁ The host is kept in a special place called the Tabernacle, behind the altar.

Children helping ▷ at the altar wear robes called vestments.

Praying alone

Sometimes Christians pray quietly to God on their own. This is a chance for them to think about what God means to them.

This man is praying in front ▷
of a special picture called
an ikon. He is making the
sign of the cross on his body.

◁ This woman is lighting
a candle and saying a
prayer while she kneels
in front of a statue of Jesus.

25

Children in a church

In many churches children help in different ways. On Sundays children can go to classes where they learn about being Christians and hear stories from the Bible.

◀ These children are making models as part of learning about a story from the Bible.

◁ Children from a nearby school are in this church choir.

Often children read ▷
from the Bible during
a service.

Glossary

altar	a special table in a church on which Holy Communion or Mass is celebrated
baptized	becoming a member of the Christian church by being blessed with holy water
Bible	the special book for Christians
blessed	when God has shown someone or something a special feeling or sign of his love
church	the place where Christians go to worship God and learn about the Christian faith
choir	a group of singers in a church
congregation	the people at a service
cross	one of the signs of the Christian church because Jesus died on one
crucifix	a cross which shows Jesus on it to remind Christians of his love for them
font	a bowl to hold the water for a baptism

God	known by Christians as the Father, Son and Holy Spirit
holy	people who live their lives close to God or special Christian places and times
Holy Communion	a service that helps Christians feel close to God. In some Christian churches it is called Mass
host	a round, thin piece of special bread
hymns	songs sung to God
ikon	special religious images found in some churches
Mass	a special service that helps Christians feel close to God. In some churches it is called Holy Communion
prayers	when people listen and talk to God
saints	holy people who live a good life
service	a meeting of Christians in church

Index

Photographic acknowledgements:
Cover: Steve Shott Photography; Sonia Halliday and Laura Lushington. **Insides:** P6 Nicholas Kane/Arcaid P9 top Angela Wood P9 bottom right Carlos Reyes-Manzo, Andes Press Agency P10 Mohamad Ansar, Impact P14 Mohamad Ansar, Impact P15 Sonia Halliday, Laura Lushington P16 H. Rogers, Trip P17 The Methodist Church, Camberwell P18 Carlos Reyes-Manzo, Andes Press Agency P26 John Fryer, Circa Photo Library P27 top Mark Cator, Impact All other photographs by Steve Shott Photography. With thanks to the Russian Patriarchal Cathedral of the Dormiton and All Saints, The Church of Our Lady, Camberwell Methodist Church, and St. Edwards RC Primary School